Forever Plagued

THIS MIND OF MINE

Russell A. Ybuan

Table of Contents

Acknowledgments	ix
Despair Pollutes the Air	1
Unbroken	2
Grief Speaks	3
Cursed	4
My Memory of You Will Dissipate in Time	5
The Lethargy of Life	6
Gray Compliments Your Skin Tone	7
Heyday	8
Lips Foster Venom	9
Necrotizing	10
Doomsday	11
Dark Discovery	12
Fictional Face	13
Tears and Fears	14
Oakland Umbrellas	15
My Only Request	16
Funeral Dreams	17
A Hidden Treasure	18
Play Pretend	20

Petals in Tears	21
The Alt Factor	22
Particles of Your Horror Show	23
She Defined Suicide	24
The Aesthetics of Black	25
Cemetery Picnic	26
Light-Years Today	27
Dark Softness	28
A Friendly Reminder	29
I Clap When You Say Something Good	30
Creative Ashes	31
In a State of Decline	32
Nightmare	33
A Moment of Bliss	34
My Armageddon	35
Dialogue Left with Breath	36
Departure	37
Coffins Continue to Pour	38
Contrast of Black	39
Interstellar Haze	40
Enjoy Life	41
Outbound Empire	42
Random Thoughts	43
My End	44
Regretful Failure	45
Life Was Toasty	46
Eve of Ending	47
Change	49

Ghost Town	50
The Greatest Mystery	51
The Pearl in You	52
Painless Days	53
It Rains with Drought	54
The Damned 10 Percent	56
The Miniscule	57
Irate World	58
Dead End	59
Broken Arrows	60
Unforgiving Pain	61
The End of Us	62
Hiatus	63
Adapt to Cope	64
Cardboard Box	65
Fractured Lies	66
False Smiles	67
I Wear This Watch Only Because of You	68
Pause	69
Listen Please	70
Time Is My Enemy	71
Moth-Ridden Wind	73
A Funeral of Strangers	74
Free Roses	75
Maribel	76
Ambiguous	77
I Can't Remember	78
Nyctophilia	79

Beheading	80
Chaos in Disguise	81
Disappointment Is Impending	82
Smile	83
Solitude	84
Abstract Stranger	85
You Win the Trophy	86
Evening's Fall	87
Malevolence Is Becoming of Her	88
My Eyes Belong to You	89
It Never Fails	90
Prescription of You	91
One Hundred Thousand Pounds	92
Dark Lights the Sky	93
Black Hole of Today	94
Anonymous	95
My Unforeseen Introduction of You	96
Marisha	97
Breath Leaves as You Arrive	98
The Wooden Box	99
Decibel	101
Last-Minute Stranger	102
Forget November	103
Allegory of My Life	104
Sounds of Scythes	105
About the Author	107

Acknowledgments

THANK YOU TO my sister, Ethel—those six words you told me that dismal night have made the biggest difference in my life. I wouldn't know what I'd do without you. Manuel—the most handsome guy I know, it was your concise interpretation of the popular children's story that inspired the bleak cover art of this book. Frank—our endless talks inspire me in so many ways, and remember, I will always persevere as oil goes to the squeaky wheel. Gail and Tracy—despite the distance, you two have always remained close to me, especially when I was at my lowest. I appreciate you both so much. Harry—always keeping it real while living life deep in the "Dino". Jewn—cheers to not being found in a ditch and living a better heyday every day. Indra—you add so much color and life to my dark world, I miss you with all my heart. Jared, Andrew, and Kris—my Oakland riders for life. If it wasn't for mosquitos, I never would've met any of you and experience all those fuzzy but awesome moments. Dre—my last tattoo belongs to you because I got muffin to lose. Jack—for the genuine support and open ears. Gabe and Stephanie—for providing the creative and inspiring vacancy. A very special thank-you to Nicole—you are the reason this book happened. You've been, and still are, an integral part of my life. You had me at madball.

Despair Pollutes the Air

A funeral hymn
Endless screams of grief; vile howls
This is my life now

Unbroken

You pushed me into the abyss.
I fell tumbling down this bottomless pit.
Withdrawn completely from that life, only my shadow remains.
Trickles, then drops, the last flickering light blown out.
The grayness darkened.
The night fell heavy.
The sound of its wrath grew interminable to nothingness.
I lay on my back carelessly,
helpless to the unrelenting violence of the storm.
I drown instantly, and I drown again.
The struggle repeats itself in an endless succession of suffering.
Left for dead in this void, unbroken.

Grief Speaks

I stand at this execution line,
blinded with cloth,
instilled in grief.
The laughter of the betrayers.
The scent of death speaks.
A stench of forgiveness.
The redolence of life.
Moments before I'm thrown
deep into my grave—
closer to home—
only in dreams of hope.

Cursed

Against my will, she planted this seed.
It grew this undying longing.
Forever cursed in my personal hell.
My heart burns only for her.

My Memory of You Will Dissipate in Time

There was a time when I cherished each
   moment I spent with you.
It was during that time when I became
   incredibly anxious without you.
I remember a time when nothing else
   mattered but you.
It took me some time to realize you were only
   an illusion.

The Lethargy of Life

The desolate and dry pain of waking up after
    a failed attempt at ending.
Left alive, ridden of dread, teased by the near
    sight of infinite blackness.
Tears of cruelty crumble away; love cheats,
    leaves, dissolves, and dies.
The aftermath of loneliness. Decades of
    mental decay.
The crowds of blurry faces, these strangers
    continue to walk through
the emptiness of my existence.

Gray Compliments Your Skin Tone

Your existence is my obsession.
Your indifference results in my gradual decay.
Those beautiful glossy eyes.
That delicate quivering face.
The sound of your enchanting muddled
    screams
makes you IRRESISTIBLE.
That duct tape compliments your skin tone.

Heyday

The best times of my life were when I was a
    kid.
I should've died by the time I turned twelve.

Lips Foster Venom

One stare.
A quick gaze.
Our first kiss.
Those venomous lips.
This wanderlust of yours
was immediately injected
within each vessel.
A permanent mark
on my anatomical heart.
My only reminder
of those lost
moments of yesterday.

Necrotizing

Lost from light.
Stuck inside an endless maze.
I've sunk too deep,
trapped against my will.
But I continue to inject death;
I've lost all will.
I feel myself withering away
into a walking skeleton.
My self-inflicted decay.

Doomsday

I should've perished that night but
the eloquence of your eyes
suggests the reason why I'm still alive.

Dark Discovery

I'd rather wander through the dark unknown among murky shadows and discover real love than to settle for anything less in the shining and beaming sun.

Fictional Face

That blurry evening among crowds of
    strangers,
surrounded by the drunken banter and loud
    noise,
was the moment I saw you,
a girl with a smile of intrigue that appeared
    out of thin air.
Within moments, we stood face-to-face,
intimate in proximity; we exchanged
    randomness.
The night grew full of fuzz, slurred and
    forgotten words.
But one thing I remember as clear as day
was this hypnotic attribute of yours.
Each moment you smiled,
your eyes smiled in unison—
a wondrous allure—
the only thing I recall about that evening
    blur.

Tears and Fears

Life is full of tears, fears, and exuberance.
I've found, without the heartache and sorrow,
I wouldn't know what true love is.
Experience.

Oakland Umbrellas

It's a storm of relentless violence outside;
scattered, broken umbrellas raid the streets.
As tumbleweeds roll freely in the vast valleys
    of death,
I sit underneath this bridge among the
    skeletons and villages,
while I run away to another world to escape
    the rain of reality.

My Only Request

To the pretenders
Do me this only favor
Pretend I am dead

Funeral Dreams

Existing in a trivial world saturated with
>indifference,
the monotony of living—that dreaded
>reluctance
of the nine-to-five grind—and mindless
>consumerism
and self-indulgence standing in for false
>happiness. A foreshadowing
of the end; the ashes blown away, a speck of
>dust in nothingness.
The dreams of my funeral. Death is becom-
>ing of me.

A Hidden Treasure

Of your many enthralling qualities
obvious to the naked eye
most, if not all, are quick to fall for at least
    one,
by mere sight.
But I admit, I found something worthwhile,
inconceivable and deeply rooted—
impossible to detect—

a timeless, elusive secret.

But I was clairvoyant to it

the moment you walked in my life.

Through time and unconditional love,

its luminous aura became perceptible.

Forever Plagued

I was in awe of its prismatic spark,

buried deep within a mysterious chamber of
 your heart.

I discovered this hidden treasure—

unknown to you,

of you, for you—

by pure luck,

just like the day I met you.

Play Pretend

This face I wear hides the pain of today.
Torn tear ducts, floods of hurt,
my thirst for life dried—
a plastic smile, paralyzed eyes wide open—
death unravels inside.
This fictional voice speaks the truth I write.
A fraudulent exterior, my hoax shatters every
    mirror
I see and reveals an empty costume, invisible
    inside.
My secret disclosed. I've been in disguise.
Just pretend along.
Pretend it's still me and
play ALIVE with me.

Petals in Tears

The sky pouts and splatters,
incessant tears begin to overflow the pavement with regret and gloom.
The garden outside is flooded with sorrow.
Each flower wilts away, afloat to fall prey.
Just yesterday, it was full of life. Today it has become a cemetery of dead,
drowning petals in tears from lost hope.
The sunrise falls deep behind the black shadows
during these mourning hours. I'm trapped in this frost-
embittered storm permanently; love continues to fail, and all hope
sinks deep away.

The Alt Factor

Your hazel eyes,
duchess nose,
pouty lips,
and pearly whites
can't hide
all those lies
inside that
transparent mind
of yours.

Particles of Your Horror Show

Ashes of my past
erased by the gust of
today. The blur of your
face remains;
it's all dust
in the end.

She Defined Suicide

The only regret of my life
stood in front of me,
the face of pure evil,
all the pain, agony, and misery
instantly reemerged;
until another glance
of her hypnotic smile
and captivating eyes;
I walked one step closer
to my gradual suicide.

The Aesthetics of Black

As the years fleeted by during the advent of
    adolescence—
seemingly in one wink or a couple of ticks
    and a few broken hearts—
life fell upon us. Names and faces long
    forgotten only to be replaced and buried
    underneath
an endless supply of the hardships called life.
    Despite the accumulated scars
formed beneath us both, not a year seemed to
    pass you by:
timeless is written on your smile.

Cemetery Picnic

The world would be a colorless place without
 you.
This world would remain black and gray if it
 were only me.
We're only worlds away by measurement of
 distance.
But your lucid words transcend with utter
 vibrancy;
your voice evokes a perfect, iridescent day at
 a cemetery
and resonates in my ears—an idyllic, haunt-
 ing whisper—
as if you were near. The beauty of your words
 and voice
precede a world of distance.

Light-Years Today

The rain pours outside,
but, only because of you,
the sun burns inside.

Dark Softness

The cacophonous screams
of malevolence, snarls of hostility,
and the dissonance of raw exasperation
have a tranquil way of silencing my mind.

A Friendly Reminder

A lifetime of misery was worth all the pain—
    life just got in the way.
Please tell them I missed the last train. They'll
    soon forget, but reassure
them I'm OK. I'm finally happy, even toward
    the end.

I Clap When You Say Something Good

I detest everything about you.
I uphold this false demeanor to mask my
 hatred.
A sudden glance of your repulsive face
can completely dismantle my day.
The days that I love are the nights
when I dream of your death.
I lied when I considered you as a friend.

Creative Ashes

My creative energy.
Burning to keep it alive.
It's all ashes. Dead alive.

In a State of Decline

The beauty of the color red.
A lifetime of misery leaves.
The blissfulness of my end.
I dance away from this life.
That inner pain flushes away.
As my blood floods the floor,
this bathroom becomes a murder scene.

Nightmare

You were a nightmare
in disguise that entire time,
but you continue
to haunt me in my dreams.

A Moment of Bliss

This mystery deep in your eyes
of a timeless, pallid glow.
A lonely cluster of bliss
shines a million lifetimes.
The totality of my existence.

My Armageddon

The world keeps crashing down on me.
But I'm still standing.
Barely.

Dialogue Left with Breath

That strange occurrence, instant attraction—
her body language,
those eyes, that flirtatious smile—
my initiative for conversation.
But I froze, struggled to remember
these memorized words, my dialogue left
    with breath.
Everything second nature—all the
    confidence,
witty reaction, charming nothingness, became nonexistent.
I instantly became that boy, shy, innocent,
    and scared.
Inferior in every sense.
A reminder of a feeling lost years ago
all because of that girl
I wish I'd known.

Departure

A piece of myself is gone forever.
This emptiness increases.
The pain inside is unforgiving.
The shadow of my silhouette,
dangling on a rope.
An elegant reminder:
with death, pain escapes.

Coffins Continue to Pour

It'll forever rain days of tears.
The unexpected gloom, cheer,
excitement, disappointment,
and all the opposites.
However, the coffins continue to pour.
The slow, gradual march to our demise.
But something about today, I was
reminded how intense it felt to feel alive,
despite the dread of death looming nearby.

Contrast of Black

You stole all the gray somberness inside
and replaced it with a contrast of light.
Life was finally on my side,
that pale evening amid a blur
of crowds, when we crossed
paths for the first time.
A moment I waited for all
my life
until all your lies
revealed your fraudulent behavior.
That moment I walked away
replaced a contrast of light
with a full spectrum.
Parasites belong in the dark,
refunds are not accepted.

Interstellar Haze

One glance of your timeless allure
and I stray away deep in space
because of your interstellar gaze.
You emit this glisten and glow
with each blink; you expose
stars, bright, of a clear midnight sky.
Your natural spectral light describes
those diamonds in your eyes.

Enjoy Life

Despite your death,
you still live in me always.
Despite your schizophrenic ways,
you taught me to live life
my own way.

Outbound Empire

This desolate and vast landscape
where the gusty winds blow
with an oppressed ferocity; the howling
sound of retribution. A direct audible reflec-
> tion of its
plagued, impoverished population and unjust
> judicial system.
A fraudulent picturesque postcard of the
> snow-covered
mountaintops within the transverse range.
> An evil
empire full of ghost towns, the walking dead,
> violence, and
the lottery of life when least expected.

Random Thoughts

These blots of thought drip
on paper as art or words;
aesthetics of blurb.

My End

My living nightmare
turned into a thousand more.
My end will never cease.

Regretful Failure

I'm still in love with you—I can't deny it;
if you only knew the truth.
But it's too late, you've moved on;
I'm only part of your past,
while you still live in my present.

Life Was Toasty

I feel nothing but numbness. I've lost the
 ability
to see
to touch
to feel
to grasp.
I have recently lost my ability to live life care-
 lessly with genuine vitality.
Somehow, I managed to lose something I as-
 sumed would always remain intact.
Somewhere along the way, I suddenly forgot
 to live.

Eve of Ending

The ominous, toxic black cloud looming. A thousand bricks falling.
On the eve of self-destruction. That predatory, malicious disease.
Cursed as a recluse. Forced to endure in solitude. That black hole
polluted with despair and torment. Forced to withstand that endless whirlwind,
unpredictable in nature. These words resonated. This person. That intensity
in her silent voice met me halfway. Our struggles mirrored each other.
Our bond instant. This innate darkness within us. A diamond in this dark cave.
That bleak place. She and I both looked death in its face. It was the mayhem,
punishment, that unknown deep-rooted pain. A mysterious, perpetual suffering
most can't comprehend. Ironically, it was the darkness of the abyss that

introduced this person, priceless, to me. She
    understands aspects of myself
most can't grasp. Until she inadvertently en-
    tered my life, I was desolate.
She's written everything I thought I only
    knew. Those words she said to me
saved me from myself—my worst enemy.
    This bond, her being, her prose,
her poems, each word I hear every day. This
    friendship, this connection
began as a stranger I was meant to know. No
    need to mention her name.
She knows each word was written just for her.
As mentioned in the beginning,
the timing was impeccable.
She introduced herself while
I was on the eve of ending.

Change

If by chance, you fail to recognize the person
    I've become—
by all means, leave me alone and let me be.
    Allow me to live.

Ghost Town

Full of emptiness,
en route to the gusty unknown,
I was introduced
to a new beginning and her false end.
A world of sand, quick goodbyes, dry eyes,
    lost hope,
toxic nights, and forgiving days.
All pretend.
The relevance of strangers
I won't forget to understand,
an aptitude of being invisible
only to be heard,
the cogency of not saying a word
as I drift away back to a foreign world.

The Greatest Mystery

One thing about women I know
is absolutely nothing at all,
and that's the beauty of them.
I'm continually intrigued by each one
in every shape and form.
My greatest mystery of all,
not to be solved.
But simply, loved.

The Pearl in You

Unaware and clueless of this,
but I think of you every single day.
Those four letters of affection
bloom to life impetuously,
along with an uncompromising feeling.
An undefined, genuine emotion,
naturally unconditional,
unbroken in time.
The timeless beauty of you.
Your meaning, quintessential.
The rare jewel in my life.
Enough to illuminate my days of dark.
As ephemeral as each thought may be,
this is how exactly you make me feel.
With just one thought of you.

Painless Days

Your name reminds me
of those perfect days
when life was painless
every single day.

It Rains with Drought

Most of that time ago,
was spent sitting, staring out a window,
patiently waiting till the rain fizzled,
but the ominous clouds of storm remained
    above,
produced not a drizzle but an onslaught of
    tears,
sorrow flooded the streets, overflowing
    sadness.
A season of my life.
Until you splashed light, drenched me with
    your being,
that dead feeling inside instantly awoke with
    life,
my heart pulsed intensely, and I felt the
    warmth of blood,
a rage of love dilated the narrow coronary
    tunnels,
color was added to my black-and-gray world.

But at a moment's notice, I felt that familiar pain,
my heart attacked again, what I thought was genuine,
resulted in a malignant disease, an infection told by you,
this feeling wasn't reciprocated, you instantly shattered
vitality, proved love was cruel, deserted in pieces,
torment within, heated, a mirage of you continually appears
in vast emptiness, left in a drought of misery.
Seasons of my abysmal life.

The Damned 10 Percent

Positivity
Is my goal of today, hell
Never mind, I fail

The Miniscule

The constant frustration
and lack of patience
over the miniscule
is how I deal with life
without you.

Irate World

I don't want to know what her "life expectancy rate" is.
It makes me irate to hear this, so I'd rather not know.
How am I supposed to feel OK, knowing this?
I expect her to live a longer life minus all the tears.
Instead, you gave me a timeline of my biggest fear.

Dead End

This road I'm on
Is one long descent
Wind in my hair
Sun blinding my eyes
Screams of excitement
Holding her hand
With a firm grasp
Not unlike the first time
As the descent continues
The sun quickly disappears
Wind thickened of fog
She screams in terror
Then vanishes in the frostbitten air
Sheer fear takes over
I'm alone in darkness again
This endless drop continues
Pummels chaotically
Until I hit rock bottom
Lost and alone
In a place, unknown

Broken Arrows

Two arrows traveling at the speed of life.
Side by side with a trajectory of a natural line.
An entire year passes with fervent velocity,
through the buzz and whirl, each moment we
    shared,
I recall with accurate precision. That unex-
    pected, wondrous time.
But somehow, for reasons unknown, that cold
    blade of yours,
snaps me in half, you turn your back and flee
    during a time I need you most,
the closest person in my life, chose to be the
    most distant
while I'm coping with this crisis on my own.
    Those words you wrote,
everything you said is meaningless. The
    meaning of you already left,
you're still here but we're already worlds away.
    From love to nothing,
our story came to a sad end.

Unforgiving Pain

I hate that pain
When it hits
It stabs and stings
Abruptly, unexpectedly
But it's only temporary
Crying, I've found,
is my only solution
It's become a normality

The End of Us

You tell me this is the end of you?
Little do you know, I've been
deteriorating with you.

Hiatus

I hate this
Reality I'm stuck in
I'm in dire need
Of a Hiatus
Life loves to rain on me
It's not fair, it makes no sense
She doesn't deserve this
Please take me instead
I beg
Do not take her away from me
My life is empty as is

Adapt to Cope

Only visible in my own privacy
I let it all out at the beginning of my day
These tears of despair flow without restraint
Another transition, this deep inner pain
A numbness to reality
This different struggle
Completely unknown to me
It's magnitude, life shattering
Hearing those dreaded words
That moment my heart crumbled
Into a thousand pieces
It was when my perception changed,
This paradoxical world

Cardboard Box

My life inside a box.
The ability to unravel
the mysterious world.
But I remain restrained
as the burning flames
wither and wave
goodbye
uncontrollably.
My life within a box;
love confines me here.

Fractured Lies

Your doubt only fuels
My passion of rage inside
Suicidal heart

False Smiles

A part of me blocked out
The seriousness of everything
Just to sustain some normalcy
In this unforgiving world
While I crumble inside
Trying my best to conceal
This ruthless thing called
      Life
Covered with false smiles
My shadow of existence
Specks of light disappear in time

I Wear This Watch Only Because of You

I sit here in the dark on my way home,
some hundreds of miles away from you
every minute, every second slides away
in this hourglass of sorrow instilled in my
    mind.
I deprive myself of sleep from losing any
    time.
It's the only thing I can do to keep you alive.

Moth-Ridden Wind

The day brings death
as the night falls heavy of life.
The chronic struggle escapes,
tears of utter ambivalence
precipitates the somber state
of the fog-enriched air,
aesthetic in nature,
you fly blindly into the nocturnal sky,
a butterfly flutters away
through the moth-ridden wind.
The silent *thank-yous* and
quiet *goodbyes* induce
the clear midnight darkness,
as constellations glow
of brighter days ahead.

A Funeral of Strangers

Forlorn in a world of strangers and unfamiliar faces. Its grim vastness; a place of passive nature and docile behavior. The light shines heavy despite darkness, as I witness the sight of a funeral procession.

Free Roses

The redolence of roses on an empty grave.
A requisite included on my simplistic,
paperless will. Trust dwindles, dissolves, and
obliterates, courtesy of the intermittent
impostors the forecast of tomorrow negates.

Maribel

You reminded me
things can still be beautiful
in a state of fog and haze.

Ambiguous

The ambiguousness of you
has become a mystery
impossible to solve.
I gravitate toward you,
the relative unknown.

I Can't Remember

I can't remember
your name
your face
your voice
your scent.
All I can remember is that exhilarating
feeling when you were still here.

Nyctophilia

Nocturnal in thought
I feel alive once night falls.
In darkness, I thrive.

Beheading

The abomination of my self-inflicted
 retribution.
In a valley twilight of torment and vileness.
The grief-stricken stone where blood seeps
 incessantly.
My own mother endlessly weeps from
 despair,
another victim fallen with overwhelming
 despondency.
This mental plague of atrocity.

Chaos in Disguise

The beautiful phenomena of your eyes.
Each thought of you becomes a theory
of surprise.

Disappointment Is Impending

And yet, here we have another one. Another one to excite, to entice, to admire, to adore. Another to be in awe of. Another to explore, to discover. Another to become smitten with, to share moments with. Another that imbues. Another to amuse. Another one that ends up having no clue. Another one to lose patience for, to lose all logic for. Another one to ignore. Another one that falls too fast in love. Another one to grow weary of. Another one to frustrate, to confuse, to anger, to ignite, and yet, another one to eventually lose.

Smile

You remind me
of the beauty of life
when you expose
the alluring glow
of the morning sky
each time you smile.

Solitude

As far as I could remember, I never did enjoy being placed in a room full of people a room full of observers and spectators. I never knew why I've always felt nervous around people I don't know. I never could figure out why. I've always felt nervous around people I do know. Sometimes I wish I was placed in a world full of strangers. I am. I was.

Abstract Stranger

Her seductive lips paint hints of chaos
when an initial thought becomes a theory.
The unpredictable turbulence of her
creative behavior and its equivalence
to fractal mathematics on canvas is puzzling.
Her intricate, beautiful mind is a
science of surprise—she's a pre-work
of art; a masterpiece in the making.

You Win the Trophy

I have an urge to stomp on your face until it
    disappears,
sew your mouth shut tight with thread,
and wrap a piece of rope around your neck.
There are few things I can't stand in life;
you just happen to be number one on my list.

Evening's Fall

Seeing the glimmer of your eyes that night
    was the evening I fell for you.
Years later, I still haven't fully recovered, and
    I never will.

Malevolence Is Becoming of Her

Temptation exudes through her predatory
 glare.
A perilous interaction with this bourgeois
 pretender.
A soulless mannequin, enraptured by deceit.
Her venom flows deep within my veins.
She's the inevitable
end of me.

My Eyes Belong to You

My eyes were glued to you—at first sight.
My eyes protrude for you—like in the cartoons.
My eyes belong to you—floating in a glass jar.

It Never Fails

Each moment I see you
is reminiscent of the first.
The speech in me is instantly lost.
Each fleeting kiss
becomes a quiet reminder
"the one" does exist.
The only girl that has proven to me
true love can be untarnished.
You've been in my life
for an entire decade,
yet the irresistibility of you remains.

Prescription of You

I feel sick, I've become excessively ill.
I have this sickness; it's a serious disease.
It's a life-threatening, chronic condition.
I need a remedy, my medication.
All I need is a prescription of you.

One Hundred Thousand Pounds

For all I'm worth,
I'm nothing without
the only person priceless
to me.

Dark Lights the Sky

As the ultraviolet rays
of sunlight escape,
the nocturnal shine
of the twilight sky arrives.
The quiet howls of the deprived
echo continuously, while shadows of the
suppressed roam freely along the mist.

Black Hole of Today

The warmness of light
Lost in the darkness of life
Temporarily

Anonymous

The cluster of bright dots
in the dark sky
aren't stars;
they're residuals
of a forgotten lifetime
worth a thousand lies.

My Unforeseen Introduction of You

An expeditious descry of her dainty face—
attractive in the most natural sense—
a brief conversation in relation to nothing
    worthwhile,
her voice subdued yet idyllic and delicate.
A prompt departure after an informal
    introduction,
how this transient encounter with her
felt reminiscent of an unknown, known,
    something of the other.

Marisha

The only person who brings light
in moments of bleary solitude.
Her words speak of paradisiacal warmth
that afternoon in June.
The fleeting diorama of yesterday remains
despite the gloomy clouds during this lucent
    day.

Breath Leaves as You Arrive

The very moment I see you appear,
your witchcraft takes hold of me.
The clamor of excitement surges inside,
instantly at a loss for words.
My heart aches impatiently
as it beats with violence.
Nervousness holds me captive.
The sight of opportunity lost in one second;
hesitation leads to failure yet again.
Release me from this spell immediately.
Please take pity on my decaying heart.
I detest your hypnotic curse of witchery.
Your beauty is the only cure for me.

The Wooden Box

That feeling when I left,
I didn't quite anticipate it.
As I was sitting at the table,
staring at the clock
with my bags fully packed,
moments before I had to leave,
I felt this sudden trepidation,
dreading each passing minute,
disinclined to say goodbye
while you were beside me.
When I spoke of becoming lost
in the recent past,
it was in reference to you.
What I knew then is what I know now,
the last time you saw me before I walked out
    the door
was the very last time you would ever see me.
All those thoughts, feelings, and raw
    emotions

I felt for you, I held close to me, but I can't
    hold
them anymore; I gave them back to you
in that wooden box you found in your room.
It has everything I wrote,
never meant to be read.
That wooden box was my way
of saying goodbye
without saying a word.

Decibel

This delicate exuberance,
a rarity I sense within you,
a person unknown with an ability
to evoke beauty of the highest decibel
yet restrain it all in quiet confidence.
This nervousness.
A sense I retain from one thought of you.
I wish I could've met you
at a different place in time,
another life, or not at all.

Last-Minute Stranger

The distance from this last-minute stranger.
Her introduction during the cusp of an ending.
The games that life plays on us,
timing is never of the essence.
She was only perfect
because I had to walk the opposite direction.

Forget November

I just want to leave.
Tell me why I'm even here.
Everything I know and love
will eventually leave.
I'm already falling
but I'm still here.
I think I was born in fall
with all the dead leaves.
I think I'll wait till fall,
when I'll finally leave.

Allegory of My Life

For all that I've said,
everything I've done.
The wrongs and rights,
these decisions in life.
All my mistakes,
these constant hardships;
the consequences paid
with full interest,
my state of mind,
the strength conjured inside.
These junctions in life
took me on my own path.
Introduction.
Chapter one.
And so it begins.
This allegory of my life.

Sounds of Scythes

The inevitable day of dread,
the quietus sound of the sinister scythe,
marks the day when I disappear from this earth.
The dearly departed, this time of sorrow, a cloak of darkness,
during a day of mourning, the air heavy from anguish.
My body cremated into ashes.
The day of my death finally came.
Although my purpose in life fulfilled,
immortalized, so no need for despair.
Wipe each of your tears,
for the memory of my name
is neither dead nor gone,
as my cathartic voice and
words will live and carry on.

About the Author

Russell A. Ybuan is a writer from Oakland, California, who has confronted in his work many emotional and personal obstacles. *Forever Plagued* is his first collection of poetry.

Made in the USA
Las Vegas, NV
22 April 2022

47840652R00069